D1279454

THE MIDDLE AGES

Library Edition published 1989
Published by Marshall Cavendish Corporation
147 West Merrick Road
Freeport, Long Island
N.Y. 11520

Typeset by Jamesway Graphics
Hanson Close Middleton Manchester M24 2HD
Printed in the USA by Worzalla Publishing
Company, Wisconsin

LIBRARY OF CONGRESS
Library of Congress Cataloging-in-Publication
Data

The Middle Ages.
    p. cm. — (Exploring the past: 2)
    Bibliography: p.
    Includes index.
    Summary: Describes the lives and times of
William the Conqueror, Richard I, and King
John.
    ISBN 0–86307–995–4: $19.95.
    ISBN 0–86307–993–8 (set): $119.95
    1. Great Britain — History — Medieval
period, 1066-1485 — Biography — Juvenile
literature. 2. Great Britain — Kings and rulers
— Biography — Juvenile literature. 3. William
I, King of England, 1027 or 8-1087 — Juvenile
literature. 4. Richard I, King of England.
1157-1199 — Juvenile literature. 5. John, King
of England, 1167-1216 — Juvenile literature. [1.
Great Britain — History — Medieval period,
1066-1485. 2. William I, King of England, 1027
or 8-1087. 3. Richard I, King of England,
1157-1199. 4. John, King of England, 1167-1216.
5. Kings, queens, rulers, etc.] I. Marshall
Cavendish Corporation. II. Series.
DA177.M5 1989
942.02 — dc 19   88–21644
                                              CIP
                                              AC

ISBN 0–86307–993–8 (set)
ISBN 0–86307–995–4 (vol)

The Middle Ages is number two in the Exploring
the Past series.

Credits: Front cover: Susan Moxley;
page 3: Nick Harris

THE MIDDLE AGES

William the Conqueror

Richard the Lionheart

King John

Marshall Cavendish

NEW YORK · TORONTO · LONDON · SYDNEY

STAFF LIST

Series Editor
Sue Lyon

Assistant Editors
Laura Buller
Jill Wiley

Art Editor
Keith Vollans

Production Controller
Tom Helsby

Managing Editor
Alan Ross

Editorial Consultant
Maggi McCormick

Publishing Manager
Robert Paulley

British Library

Titles in the EXPLORING THE PAST series

READER'S GUIDE

The Bridgeman Art Library

Imagine that you owned a time machine, and that you traveled back to the days when your parents were in school. Your hometown and school would look different, while the clothes, music, and magazines that your parents were enjoying might seem odd, perhaps amusing, and certainly "old fashioned" and "out of date." Travel back a few hundred years, and you would be astonished and fascinated by the strange food, homes, even language, of our ancestors.

Time machines do not yet exist, but in this book you can explore one of the most important periods of the past through the eyes of three people who made history happen. An introduction sets the scene and highlights the significant themes of the age, while the chronology lists important events and when they happened to help you to understand the background to the period. There is also a glossary to explain words that you may not understand and a list of other books that you may find useful.

The past is important to us all, for the world we know was formed by the actions of people who inhabited it before us. So, by understanding history, we can better understand the events of our own times. Perhaps that is why you will find exploring the past so exciting, rewarding and fascinating.

CONTENTS

Graham Humphries

INTRODUCTION

The years between about A.D. 1050 and A.D. 1250 are usually called the High Middle Ages. This was the time when medieval life reached its fullest, most typical development. (Medieval just means "belonging to the Middle Ages.") But as a whole, the Middle Ages lasted for much longer – from about 800 to 1500, beginning in the "Dark Ages" and ending with the Renaissance on the threshold of modern times.

Medieval society was organized in a way which we find strange, but which suited disturbed and relatively primitive conditions. In the early Middle Ages, Europe emerged from centuries of devastating wars and tribal wanderings. It was a poor society in which most people just about managed to live by farming. Towns were small, communications bad, and trading contacts very limited. In these conditions, individuals could not rely on a distant, slow-moving royal power to maintain law and order, and, as a result, new social arrangements came into being. Taken all together, they are known as feudalism, or the feudal system.

The Feudal System
The basis of feudalism was a kind of contract by which a poorer or weaker person agreed to recognize a stronger or richer one as his lord. The lord offered his protection and granted land (known as a fief) to his new dependant, who became his vassal. In return, the vassal pledged his faith (swore fealty), became the lord's "man" (paid homage) and agreed to perform certain important services for him.

The same thing happened at every level of society, so that each lord became the vassal of a still more powerful lord. In this way, chains of lordship and service were created that ran

right up to the king. In theory, the monarch was the owner of the entire kingdom, and the greatest of his nobles, known as tenants-in-chief, were his vassals, holding their vast lands in return for the services they performed.

The most important of a vassal's services was to provide fighting men. Each tenant-in-chief agreed to spend a fixed amount of time with the king, accompanied by a certain number of knights; this was possible because each vassal of a tenant-in-chief supplied a smaller number of knights, which he obtained in turn from his vassals; and so on. The bottom place in the chain was occupied by the knight himself, who was settled on his lord's land and was supported by the work of the local peasants.

These elaborate arrangements were needed because, for hundreds of years, the knights were the most important elements in any army. Clad in full armor and mounted on a

8

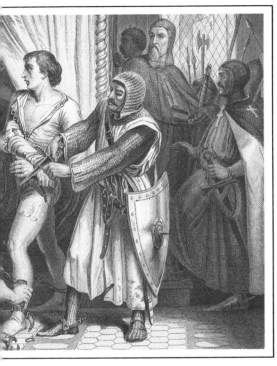

massive horse – a specially-bred steed, much bigger than the horses that were used for plowing fields – a knight could crash into an enemy with shattering effect, as the soldiers of Saladin discovered to their cost during the Third Crusade. In fact, the mounted man was the tank of the Middle Ages – a terror to foot soldiers, and almost invulnerable, even when he was alone. When he was massed with other mounted knights and charging against the foe, he was irresistible. But, in a poor society, man, armor and big horse were ruinously expensive to maintain in large numbers. In a sense, the entire feudal system was a clever arrangement for supporting knights by distributing them all over the country!

The Medieval Church
The other great institution of the Middle Ages was the Christian Church, which in western and central Europe

Sonia Halliday

meant the Catholic Church headed by the Pope in Rome. The influence of Christian belief was felt in every area of European life, so much so that the Middle Ages have also been called "the Age of Faith." The building of large numbers of churches, cathedrals and monasteries showed how intensely many believers felt, and over the centuries the Church grew enormously wealthy and powerful. On the other hand, no one was allowed to disagree with it, so it is hard to know just how devout people actually were. Most villagers, unable to read or write, probably had a garbled notion of Christian doctrine, and most may have believed in pagan superstitions and practices.

Because the Church owned vast estates and wielded so much influence, it was deeply involved in many matters that had nothing to do with religion. As a great landowner, it was part of the feudal system, as involved as any nobleman in getting and giving. It also had a political role. Leading churchmen took part in governing kingdoms; in many instances they did their work well, but sometimes ambition got the better of them. This was true even of the popes; some of them tried to gain as much territory and power as they could, quarreling with the rulers of European countries and using their spiritual authority as a political weapon. Other churchmen simply set out to enjoy life, neglecting their duties and sometimes taking advantage of simple people to get money out of them. As a result, the Church showed two different faces: it was frequently grasping and oppressive, yet it also produced inspired leaders and respected and revered holy men such as St. Francis of Assisi. In both instances, it made a deep impact on European life.

Ties of Loyalty

Because there was no strong central authority, feudal nobles and churchmen enjoyed a great deal of independence. Under a weak or unlucky king they could get completely out of hand, and the history of the Middle Ages is full of rebellions and civil wars. In England, kings were relatively powerful, because King William I was able to organize the government of the country as he wished immediately after conquering it. Even so, the English barons resisted the attempts of a later king, Henry II, to expand royal justice, and they checked King John's ambitions by having a charter of liberties – the Magna Carta – written into the law of the land.

Wars between kings could put a great strain on feudal loyalties, since it was not always clear where a man's duty lay. Through inheritance, marriage or conquest he might well own properties in different countries and might therefore be the vassal of two or more lords. If they quarreled, which should he fight for? The problem arose even at the highest level. As King of England, William the Conqueror acknowledged no earthly superior; but as the Duke of Normandy he owed loyalty and service to the King of France. In theory, the King of France might call on William of Normandy to help him wage war on William of England! For lesser men, the choice of sides was not just a matter of conscience – it could put at risk everything they owned in one country or another. And on occasion the choice was final: when King John lost all of Normandy to the King of France, his barons had to decide whether to save their English or their Norman lands by settling in one place or another and serving one of the two kings.

In time, this decision would make them into Frenchmen or Englishmen; but during the Middle Ages, this sense of nationality hardly existed. The holdings of kings and nobles crossed boundaries, and members of the Church formed an international community. By contrast, the common people were entirely local-minded: the only feeling resembling nationalism was dislike and suspicion of "foreigners," whether they were merchants from another country or just citizens from a nearby village.

The main reason for this narrow outlook was that most people never traveled. In fact, most of them were not allowed to. They were serfs, or villeins – not quite slaves, but peasants who were tied to the soil. Generally speaking, each country was divided into manors – estates that consisted of a village or two and land for farming. The lord of the manor allowed his serfs to cultivate part of the land for their own use, but, in return, they paid him heavily in goods and services; in fact, the labor of the serf sustained the entire feudal system.

A Time of Change

The general features of the High Middle Ages remained much the same for centuries. But this does not mean that nothing changed; in fact, the period was one of tremendous vitality and considerable progress. By A.D. 1000 Europe was recovering from the ravages inflicted by the last of the pagan invaders – the Scandinavian Vikings and the Magyars (Hungarians), both of whom had accepted Christianity and settled down. The forces of Christianity's great rival, Islam, remained formidable, but the Muslim grip on Spain was weakening, so the immediate threat to Europe from outside had passed.

With the release of the pressure, a rapid expansion took place. Populations increased and new lands were brought into cultivation. Towns started to grow larger and, urged on by craft and merchant guilds (associations), asserted their independence from local lords. Major trade routes developed through the Baltic and Mediterranean Seas and across Europe. Money was more widely used, and the first great banking houses were founded by Italian financiers.

Although they were launched for mainly religious reasons, the Crusades also reflected the European urge to expand – and, for nobles and knights without fiefs, the urge to acquire lands of their own. In the long run, the Crusaders failed to keep the Holy Land under Christian control; but thanks to their contact with Islamic civilization, they brought back new products, skills, and ideas from the East.

The High Middle Ages were also a time of learning and culture. The first universities – among them Oxford and Cambridge – were founded. There was little scientific progress, but advances were made in medicine. And a line of great thinkers, such as Peter Abelard and St. Thomas Aquinas, created a distinguished tradition of philosophy.

Developments during the High Middle Ages greatly improved the quality and potential of medieval life, further enhanced in the later Middle Ages (1250-1500). But that is a different, equally fascinating, story.

William
the Conqueror

William I was a remarkable man. He not only defeated his many enemies to secure his hold on his duchy of Normandy; he also conquered the strong, independent Anglo-Saxon kingdom of England. But, as well as being a great soldier, William was a strong ruler, introducing new systems of justice and land tenure, and replacing the native nobility with a new Norman ruling class. In fact, the Conquest was a true turning point, and, as the High Middle Ages began, England and the rest of Europe began a new chapter of history.

Guillmuf Regis

Peter Roberts

William's ruthlessness and courage made him a great warrior, but he was also a devout man who ruled wisely, if harshly.

One autumn day in the year 1028, close to the great castle of Falaise in Normandy, a young woman called Herleve gave birth to a healthy son. Herleve named her baby William (in French, Guillaume), and perhaps she dreamed that one day he might be a great lord—though she herself was just a simple tanner's daughter. For the baby's father was Robert, the fifth Duke of Normandy, who came to be known as Robert "The Devil." Yet even Herleve could never have imagined that William would grow up to conquer a kingdom and become one of the most powerful rulers in Europe.

Personal Profile

WILLIAM THE CONQUEROR

Born: Probably 1028 in Falaise, Southern Normandy.

Died: September 9, 1087.

Parents: Illegitimate son of Robert "The Devil," Duke of Normandy, and Herleve, daughter of Fulbert the Tanner.

Personal appearance: Tall and well built. Reddish hair with a firm angular jaw.

General: A brilliant general who inspired great fear in his enemies and loyalty in his men. Described as a king who "excelled in wisdom," he also ruled with a rod of iron. He was articulate and persuasive, devout in his religious beliefs, and constant to his friends.

EDWARD THE CONFESSOR (right) was King of England between 1042 and 1066. He liked the Normans so much that he is said to have named William as his successor, providing the basis for William's claim to the English throne. Edward was a deeply religious man and founded Westminster Abbey. This stained glass window of him is in Winchester Cathedral.

Ronald Sheridan

BATTLE DRESS

Royal Armouries

MAIL SHIRTS (left) were made from interlinking iron rings with riveted ends. Chain mail was so valuable that it was often removed from dead soldiers on the battlefield and worn again.

Among the essential items which William's fleet carried over to England were suits of chain mail for the men to use in battle. When worn over a quilted undershirt, this flexible armor provided some protection against the arrows and swords of the enemy, but only the rich warriors could afford a complete suit.

REMOVING ARMOR (left) Mail armor was a real struggle to take off without help from a friend or valet.

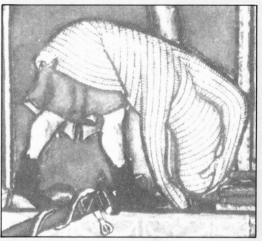

Ronald Sheridan

THEIR PLACE IN HISTORY

BC   AD
1400 1350 1300 | 400 350 300 200 150 100 50 ● | 700 750 800 850 900 950 1000 1050 1100 1150 1200 1250 1300 1350

Tutankhamen
Alexander the Great
Hannibal
Julius Caesar
Cleopatra
Charlemagne
Alfred the Great
William the Conqueror
Minamoto Yoritomo
Richard the Lionheart
King John
Marco Polo

In the Christian world, year dates are worked out from the birth of Jesus Christ. All years *after* His birth are known as AD. This stands for Anno Domini – in the year of our Lord. All years *before* His birth are known as BC – which stands for Before Christ.

There was a danger, though, that he might never grow up at all, for all through his childhood he was in constant peril. The problem was that Herleve and Robert were never married. Yet Duke Robert insisted on naming William as his heir, for he had no other sons. When the Duke died of a fever on his way home from a pilgrimage to Jerusalem in 1035, seven-year-old William became Duke, which the other Norman lords deeply resented.

William's enemies tried desperately to get rid of him,

and Normandy was plunged into bitter civil war. The young Duke had many narrow escapes, once fleeing from a castle in the dead of night and riding through the dark at breakneck speed. Yet he was both lucky and tough, and he survived. By the time he was 20, he was an experienced soldier and leader, loyal to his friends, but ruthless with his enemies.

It was the young Duke himself whose whirling sword helped put the rebels to flight at the famous battle of Val-ès-Dunes near Caen in 1047. After the battle, William imposed the rather odd Truce of God. Under this Truce, no one but William and the King of France was allowed to fight wars between Wednesday evening and Monday morning and during Lent and Advent.

Soon, William faced another threat—from the powerful Count of Anjou, Geoffrey Martel, in the south. But, in a fierce attack, William's armies captured the town of Alencon. They then hacked off the legs and arms of those who had mocked William as "the tanner," which so frightened Martel's allies that they surrendered.

By now, William was known far and wide as a brilliant, though ruthless, war leader. It was about this time that the English King, Edward the Confessor, came

THE CORONATION OF WILLIAM *William was crowned King of England in the new Westminster Abbey on December 25, 1066.*

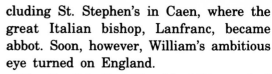

LANFRANC OF PAVIA (below) An Italian scholar, Lanfranc was a great friend of William's.

to stay in Normandy and named William, so said his friends, as heir to the English throne. A little while later, William married Matilda of Flanders — much to the annoyance of the Pope, who forbade the match, and the King of France, who felt the Duke was getting a little above himself. Even little Matilda, just four feet tall and 17 years old, was annoyed; it is said that she only accepted William once he had thrashed her a few times. Surprisingly, her husband was to prove unusually loyal.

Anxious to cut William down to size, Henry I, the French King, sent an army to Normandy. But, early one morning, as the French recovered from a night's drinking and feasting in the town of Mortemer, William launched a surprise raid and cut them to pieces.

William's enemies were now well and truly beaten and the dukedom was at peace. He and Matilda took the opportunity to found more than 20 new monasteries, in-cluding St. Stephen's in Caen, where the great Italian bishop, Lanfranc, became abbot. Soon, however, William's ambitious eye turned on England.

The English Earl Harold of Wessex had once come to Normandy and sworn an oath of loyalty to William, accepting him as the heir to the English throne. But when the time came it was Harold, not William, who was crowned King of England when Edward the Confessor died in 1066.

William was furious and made no secret of his intention to grab the English throne from him. Throughout the spring and summer of 1066, his men worked feverishly to prepare a remarkable invasion force, building a fleet of ships which would carry not only soldiers in full armor, but also 3,000 horses and even three prefabricated wooden castles, across the channel.

At first, the wind blew from the north, preventing the Normans from sailing. Then at last, on September 27, the wind veered around to the southwest, and William's fleet sped across the channel. Three weeks later, Harold lay dead on the battlefield at Hastings, and the English were scattered to the four winds. On Christmas Day, 1066, Wil-

HAWKING A keen huntsman, William created royal forests where only he could hawk and hunt.

The Harrying of the North

In the summer of 1069, Northern England was invaded by the Norsemen yet again—only this time thousands of Anglo-Saxons, instead of fighting off invaders, sprang to their aid. Marching on York, the Norsemen and the English stormed the city and slaughtered the Normans.

Blazing with wrath, William called upon all his allies in England to help him and marched north at great speed. Surprised by the ferocity of William's advance, the Norsemen retreated from their camp on the Isle of Axholme in Lincolnshire. Soon, the Normans reached Nottingham.

From Nottingham, William advanced north toward York, sending out small troops of men far to the east and west to teach the Anglo-Saxons a lesson. Men, women, children, animals, and livestock, crop and pasture all fell to the Norman flame or sword, and Yorkshire was soon devastated.

As winter closed in, William's armies marched remorsely northward, harrying village after village and town after town in his wrath. The people of the North had paid a terrible price for their resistance, and the northern lands were reduced to waste for more than a decade.

Mary Evans

There were other rebellions against William's rule, and perhaps the most famous leader of these revolts was Hereward the Wake. In 1070, Hereward and a small group of rebels joined a force of Danish invaders, who were based in Ely. Together, they attacked the town of Peterborough and sacked the treasures of its abbey. William, fearing his domination of the area was in danger, attempted to crush the rebellion by making a peace treaty with the Danish king, Sweyn. The invaders returned to Denmark under Sweyn's orders.

Hereward, however, remained, and established his headquarters at Ely. His garrison became a refuge for many enemies of the King. Hereward led a series of rebel attacks against the King until 1071, when William captured his garrison. Most of his men surrendered, but Hereward escaped into the countryside and disappeared from history.

liam was crowned King of England in the great new abbey at Westminster.

Soon afterward, William returned to Normandy leaving his half-brother Odo, Bishop of Bayeux, and William fitzOsbern in charge. Both ruthlessly exploited the English, and let their soldiers do as they wished to the poor peasants. According to the famous *Anglo-Saxon Chronicle*, they "built castles far and wide throughout the land, oppressing the unhappy people, and things went ever from bad to worse."

By the time William returned to England late in 1067, Anglo-Saxons were up in arms across the country. With typical vigor, he marched first west to Exeter, then north to York, to crush the rebellions. By 1070 people were subdued enough for William to get down to the business of running the country.

Like Odo and fitzOsbern, William built castle after castle, first of wood, then stone, to keep the people in check. But he was determined to uphold the rule of law, punishing all wrongdoers, Norman and English alike. Many of the laws William enforced so energetically were old Anglo-Saxon ones, but he made many new ones, too. It was said that an unarmed man was safer in William's England than at any time before.

William had rewarded all those who had served him at Hastings well, with gifts of land confiscated from the

15

Michael Holford

NEW BOOKS (above) *William's reign saw the production of many new books, all penned by hand.*

THE NORMAN KINGS (top left to bottom right) *William I, William Rufus, Henry I, and Stephen.*

Geoffrey Davies

missioners finished the survey in less than a year, and all the findings were written in a large volume. People called the book "Domesday" (Doomsday), for what it recorded was so final and complete that it seemed like the records of the great biblical Day of Judgment.

Shortly after the Domesday Book was completed, William returned to Normandy, where his eldest son, Robert, was in open rebellion against him. William was no longer the fit warrior he had been. But on the battlefield, he was still a force to be reckoned with, and he led the Norman army himself. Then, as he rode victoriously into the Norman city of Mantes, his horse stumbled and he was thrown against the saddle pommel and badly injured.

For some days, he lay dying in great pain at the priory of Saint Gervais in Rouen. Practical to the last, he named his son William Rufus his successor as King of England and Robert as Duke of Normandy, despite their differences. In the early morning of September 9, 1087, to the sound of the great bell of Rouen Cathedral, William died.

English; and within ten years, there were just two English landlords in the entire country. In return, William's lords undertook to provide him with a specified number of soldiers and knights whenever the need arose. From this agreement arose the "feudal system" of land ownership.

The English were never happy under William's rule, for they were taxed heavily and frequently, to pay for the castles and for the upkeep of an army to combat the constant invasions of the Norsemen. Yet it was actually the ban on hunting that seemed to cause most bitterness. William's creation of royal forests, where he alone could hunt, such as the New Forest in Hampshire, was deeply resented—particularly as many poor farmers were evicted to make way for them.

In 1086, William called for a great survey of his entire kingdom to find out what each of his tenants-in-chief owned, right down to the last cow. Astonishingly, William's com-

Ronald Sheridan

THE LAST RESTING PLACE of William was the Abbey Church of St. Stephen in Caen. Today, a simple marble plaque marks his tomb.

Sonia Halliday

The Battle of Hastings

On a grassy ridge near Hastings, William challenged Harold in a bloody battle for the English crown.

Geoffrey Davies

Luisa Ricciarini

STARRY WARNING In February, 1066, a star (Halley's Comet) was seen. Harold was told it was a bad omen.

BUILDING BOATS for the Norman invasion (below) from the Bayeux Tapestry.

On September 28, 1066, William and his army landed on the south coast of England near Pevensey. The peasants fled in terror as ship after ship plowed through the surf and grounded with a crunch on the shingle beach. There were 777 of them altogether, each with its fearsome Viking prow, and William's large army—7,000 foot soldiers and knights with their horses—took many hours to disembark.

William had been planning his invasion for many months—ever since Harold Godwineson had been crowned King of England when King Edward the Confessor died. William felt that the crown of England should be his, not Harold's, and he was determined to take it.

Three days later, a breathless messenger came riding into York with the news to find Harold celebrating his great victory over the Norse army of Harald Hardrada. Like William, Hardrada had invaded England with a vast force, hoping to wrest the English throne from

DUKE OF NORMANDY (above) the victor of Hastings—a statue in the French town of Falaise.

Michael Holford

17

Susan Moxley

Harold. But after a heroic march north from London, King Harold caught Hardrada by surprise at Stamford Bridge in Yorkshire and defeated the Norsemen. The tidings of William's invasion was therefore a bitter blow for Harold. But he rallied his battle-weary men and set off south again at once.

Harold's men covered the 200 miles to London in just four days and, after a brief rest, marched on to meet the Normans at Caldbec Hill near Hastings. As dawn rose on Sunday October 14, the English were standing in close ranks upon the crest of the hill, watching the Normans come closer and closer up the hill.

Less than 150 yards from the English, William paused and split his army into three groups. On the left were William's Breton allies. On the right were hired troops from France and Flanders. And, in the center, were the Normans themselves.

At about nine in the morning, horns and trumpets sounded, men shouted their battle cries, and the Norman assault began. First, archers crept slowly forward, shooting volley after volley into the English line. But most arrows bounced harmlessly off the wall of English shields, and soon the Normans had run out of arrows.

Then, as the Norman infantry pressed closer, the English drew their shields together and William had to

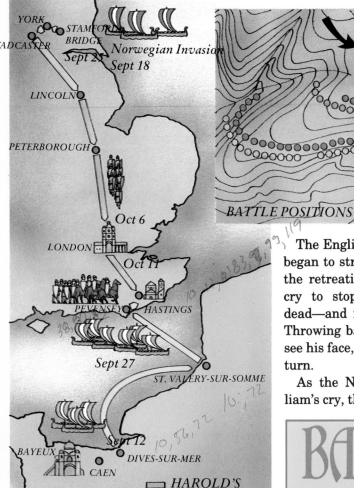

York
TADCASTER
STAMFORD BRIDGE
Norwegian Invasion
Sept 25
Sept 18
LINCOLN
PETERBOROUGH
Oct 6
LONDON
Oct 11
PEVENSEY HASTINGS
Sept 27
ST. VALERY-SUR-SOMME
BAYEUX
DIVES-SUR-MER
CAEN
Sept 12

HAROLD'S
WILLIAM'S

Harold's approach

SENLAC RIDGE

BATTLE POSITIONS

William's approach

Key:
Huscarles
English Infantry
Harold's Army
Norman Cavalry
Norman Archers
Road

The English, believing victory was theirs, began to stream down the hill in pursuit of the retreating Normans, ignoring Harold's cry to stop. But William was far from dead—and it was he who turned the tide. Throwing back his helmet so that all could see his face, he urged his dispirited troops to turn.

As the Normans swung around at William's cry, they caught the pursuing English

HAROLD'S DEATH (right) Legend has it that Harold was killed by an arrow. Historians now think that the wound wasn't fatal, but it enabled William's men to strike him down.

watch wave after wave of Norman foot soldiers struggle up the ridge, only to be repulsed by storms of spears, javelins, axes and stones.

Meanwhile, the Breton knights hurled themselves on the English right. But the assault was ragged and badly led, and they were easily beaten off by Harold's robust "huscarles," his highly trained professional foot soldiers. Demoralized, the Bretons turned and fled.

Suddenly, a terrible cry arose from the Norman center, where William was in the thick of the fighting. "William is dead!" shouted someone, as yet another horse was slain beneath the battling Duke. Horrified, the Normans began to retreat, feeling that there was little hope of victory without their leader.

BAYEUX TAPESTRY

The famous embroidery known as the Bayeux Tapestry is a series of pictures illustrating all the events surrounding the Battle of Hastings, from the reign of Edward the Confessor to the death of King Harold. It is the only work of its kind to survive from the 11th century.

The tapestry is believed to have been commissioned by William's half brother Odo, Bishop of Bayeux. It may have been made in England, as the craftsmanship of the English embroiderers was well known at the time. The designs were probably executed by an artist, then sewn by a team of needlewomen, between 1088 and 1092.

The tapestry is embroidered on a background of coarse linen fabric, using

HAELIS

Mary Evans

out in the open. There, they were slain mercilessly by William's men, while the rest of the English watched helplessly.

By now, the battle had raged for over five hours, but the English shield wall remained intact. The Norman archers launched another attack, shooting high into the air so that showers of arrows rained down on the heads of the men behind the shield wall.

Many Englishmen fell beneath the ferocious Norman onslaught, and gradually the Norman knights began to break through the English lines. The huscarles stood their ground doggedly around the King, but more and more of them fell to the heavy Norman swords. Then Harold was struck in the face by an arrow and severely wounded.

In the final charge, Harold was killed and his body grossly mutilated. The huscarles who surrounded him died at his side. The remaining English fled into the forest hoping that the failing light would cloak their escape. They were mercilessly pursued by the Normans until darkness finally fell.

yarns in eight colors. It is about 20 inches high and spans aboutt 230 feet.

Today, the tapestry is on display in Bayeux, France.

ON CAMPAIGN In this scene from the Bayeux Tapestry (below), William and Harold go on a campaign. Two soldiers are rescued by Harold from quicksand.

HAROLD'S MONUMENT (right) The spot where Harold fell at the Battle of Hastings is now marked with a stone monument. The inscription on the monument is written in French.

ET hIC: TRANSIERVNT: FLVMEN: COSN
hIC: hAROLD: DVX: TRAh
DEARENA

Michael Holford

NORMAN STRONGHOLDS

Great castles were built by the Norman conquerors to keep the rebellious English under control.

The Normans made it plain right from the start that they intended to stay in England. As they spread across the country after the Conquest, they built castle after castle to safeguard the soldiers that kept the English in check. Wherever a Norman baron had lands, or a vital strategic point to protect, up went a castle. Soon, scores of towns, villages, and valleys across the land were dominated by great Norman castles, frightening symbols of Norman might.

The sites for these castles were chosen masterfully, nestled in the bend of a river or perched high on a rocky crag. Norman engineers spent weeks locating a spot that was easy to defend and that gave a commanding view of the country around—and also had a good water supply. And if there were houses on the best site, the Normans simply demolished them, ruthlessly evicting the occupants. In Lincoln, as many as 166 houses were dismantled to make way for the castle's construction.

Norman castles, or keeps, were generally erected on top of a mound, or motte. In front of the keep, there was a forecourt or bailey, which contained a well (essential for fresh water), a hall, sleeping quarters, stabling for the horses, storerooms, and workshops. Around the outside of the motte and bailey was a wall and a deep ditch lined with great planks of wood, which were extremely difficult to climb.

Norman Achievements

The Burrell Collection

THE TOWER OF LONDON (left) was the first and greatest of all Norman castles. It was designed by a priest, Gundulph, Bishop of Rochester. The Tower stands as a monument to the strength of the Norman Conquest.

STAINED GLASS (right) was a feature of many Norman churches. Spectacular windows can still be found throughout Europe, such as this French example, which features the Prophet Jeremiah.

Timothy Woodcock

A CANDLESTICK (below) dating from about 1110.

STONEWORK (below) The Normans were great stone masons. They built beautiful vaulted ceilings, such as the nave at Durham Cathedral.

Angelo Hornak

GUNDULPH (right) was responsible for several great buildings, including Colchester Castle and Rochester Cathedral. His effigy is by the door of Rochester Cathedral.

Geoffrey Davies

DOVER CASTLE (below) was one of the first stone castles to be built after the Norman Conquest.

Bridgeman

Michael Holford

NORMAN ARCHES Many Norman churches have intricately carved entrances, like those at Kilpeck Church in Herefordshire (below left and right), Ely Cathedral (right), and Iffley Church in Oxford (far right). Some show holy scenes, others simple patterns.

Michael Holford

Angelo Hornak

Ronald Sheridan

Geoffrey Davies

Angelo Hornak

CASKET (above) This beautiful casket was a reliquary, made around 1190. Reliquaries were made to store holy relics such as the bones, hair, or belongings of saints. The sides show an enamel depiction of the stoning of St. Stephen.

The first castle to be built on English soil was at Hastings. Among the vast supplies of arms, horses, food, and drink loaded into William's fleet in Normandy were three prefabricated wooden castles, which were to serve as retreats if the battle went badly.

These castles were made in prepared sections and fitted together with wooden pegs that were stored in barrels. As soon as the fleet landed at Hastings, William's men set about finding a place to erect a castle. Their first task was to build a huge motte. The Normans were well equipped with picks and spades and skillfully made short work of this difficult task.

After the Conquest, scores of similar, but permanent, wooden castles were quickly thrown up across the country. But, although they were strongly built, the wooden castles soon rotted in the damp English climate, and there was always the risk of fire—both accidental and from the hands of unhappy

This reliquary cross shows the stonework for which the Normans were famous.

Angelo Hornak

Englishmen. So, the Normans started to build in stone.

Stone castles needed considerable planning, and usually men known as military engineers would take charge of the organization. But one man who was responsible for several great stone castles was not a military engineer at all, but a priest. Gundulph, the Bishop of Rochester, was a great friend of the king, and it was he who oversaw the building of the first great Norman castle, the keep of the Tower of London.

A wooden castle could be erected in a few months. Building in stone took much longer and demanded vast numbers of men. To build the great stone keeps, the Normans press-ganged hundreds of local people and often kept them working for many years before they could return to their farms.

Besides the laborers, the Normans had to find skilled workers. Smiths were employed to forge iron, carpenters for the necessary woodwork, and masons for the stonework. The masons worked under the supervision of the master mason, some in quarries extract-

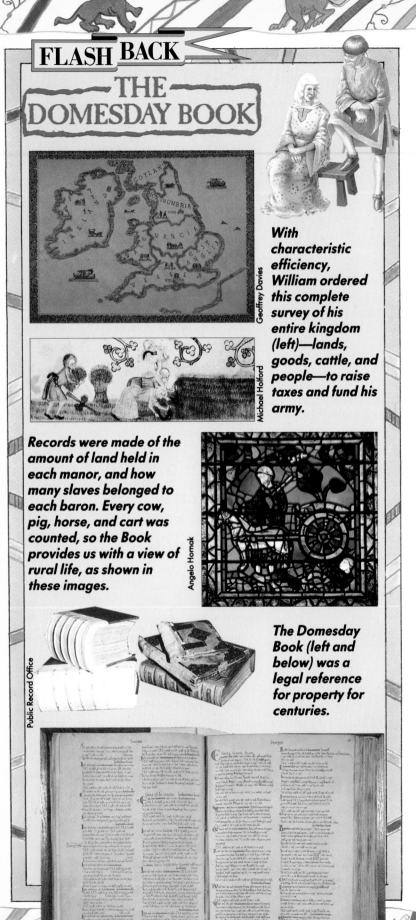

THE DOMESDAY BOOK

Geoffrey Davies

With characteristic efficiency, William ordered this complete survey of his entire kingdom (left)—lands, goods, cattle, and people—to raise taxes and fund his army.

Michael Holford

Records were made of the amount of land held in each manor, and how many slaves belonged to each baron. Every cow, pig, horse, and cart was counted, so the Book provides us with a view of rural life, as shown in these images.

Angelo Hornak

Public Record Office

The Domesday Book (left and below) was a legal reference for property for centuries.

ing the stone with large metal wedges, some cutting the blocks into suitable shapes, and some laying the blocks with mortar. In the early days of the Norman Conquest, a stone mason was never short of work!

The stone for the building had to be obtained locally or transported from another area. Transport by water was cheaper than transport by land, and stone was shipped from as far afield as Caen in Normandy. The Normans often took advantage of used materials if they were available—stones from old and crumbling Roman buildings were a particular favorite.

If the castle was built on the site of an old wooden keep, the motte had first to be leveled to give a sturdy base. Stone castles needed a good foundation of solid rock or constructed stone to build the walls. The walls themselves were built in three sections for defensive strength. The outer wall was made with skillfully cut smooth stone; the inner wall, too, was made with smooth stone; and the core in between was made with flint, inferior stone, or rubble topped with a liquid mix of mortar.

As the walls grew, wooden scaffolding was built up the sides, and carpenters and smiths set to work making pulleys and winches to raise the heavy stone blocks. The work grew harder as the laborers had to haul the stone and mortar higher. What they couldn't haul, they had to carry up the scaffolding ladders in wicker baskets. Although the scaffolding was usually sturdy, it was often wet and slippery, and the workers had to tread carefully.

Once the castle had reached its full height, the smiths and carpenters started work on the roof. This was usually made from wood and covered with lead.

Large castles could take years to build. The Tower of London was commissioned by William the Conqueror in 1078 but was not completed until 1097, ten years after his death. Although their great strongholds were built to last, the Normans could never have imagined what an enduring symbol of the conquest their castles were to become.

Richard
the Lionheart

odern historians have criticized Richard I for neglecting his country, because, during his ten-year reign, he spent only six months in England. However, in the Middle Ages, kings were not expected to be peaceful administrators; instead a true king was the epitome of knighthood – brave, noble, chivalrous and, above all, a great soldier. As his name suggests, Richard the Lionheart was all of these things. His subjects gloried in his deeds, and, when he was captured on the way home from the Crusades, they were eager to ransom their popular king.

Richard the Lionheart

Ronald Sheridan

Brave, strong and fierce, Richard I was the leader of the Third Crusade to the Holy Land. But, as a result, he neglected England.

He is one of England's most famous kings, a legendary warrior and hero, and his name has rung down through the centuries—Richard the Lionheart. Yet he could not speak English, and only spent six months in the kingdom during his ten year reign.

His father, Henry II, was an eccentric, rough person of strange temperament. Once, in a violent anger, he demanded the death of his own archbishop, Thomas à Becket, but when the man was murdered, he wept bitterly and made the priests whip him as a punishment. Eleanor of Aquitaine, Richard's mother, loathed Henry's dirty English court and encouraged her children to hate their own father. For years, Henry kept her in prison, hoping to break her power over their children.

All Europe whispered about the quarrelsome Plantagenet family and called Henry's children "the Devil's Brood" because they were so wild. They were a very powerful family. Henry II was King of England and also

Tony Masero

Personal Profile

RICHARD THE LIONHEART
Born *September 8, 1157, at Beaumont Palace, Oxford.*
Died *April 7, 1199, in Limousin, France.*
Reign *1189 to 1199.*
Parents *Henry II and Eleanor of Aquitaine.*
Personal appearance *Very tall for a Plantagenet — about 6 feet — powerfully built with auburn hair, blue eyes, and a beard.*
General *A complex man, well educated and versed in the finer arts of poetry and music. Greedy, yet at times overwhelmingly generous to his friends. Capable of great cruelty, but revered by his troops, he was famous for his courtesy and charm.*

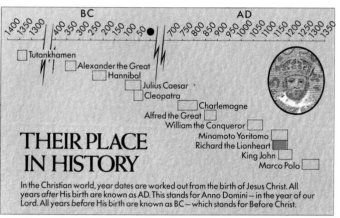

Bibliotheque Nationale

TOURNAMENTS
(left) In France, Richard went to many tournaments — mock battles in which teams of knights fought each other. This was considered serious practice for war, and Richard himself was trained as a knight.

WEALTHY LAND
Richard taxed England's wool trade (below) to fund the Crusade.

THEIR PLACE IN HISTORY

BC									AD											
1400	1350	1300	400	350	300	250	200	150	100	50	700	750	800	850	900	950	1000	1050	1100	1150	1200	1250	1300	1350

☐ Tutankhamen
☐ Alexander the Great
☐ Hannibal
☐ Julius Caesar
☐ Cleopatra
☐ Charlemagne
Alfred the Great
William the Conqueror ☐
Minamoto Yoritomo
Richard the Lionheart
King John ☐
Marco Polo ☐

In the Christian world, year dates are worked out from the birth of Jesus Christ. All years *after* His birth are known as AD. This stands for Anno Domini — in the year of our Lord. All years *before* His birth are known as BC — which stands for Before Christ.

Arxiu Mas

The Mansell Collection

BERENGARIA (left), daughter of the King of Navarre, married Richard in 1191.

controlled a vast area of France, including the rich province of Aquitaine which his wife brought him as part of her dowry.

Eleanor bore Henry seven children, and Richard was her second son. He was, from the start, her favorite boy and was brought up in her French court at Poitiers. As a small child, he watched with wonder the grand jousting tournaments where knights displayed their strength. He heard the French poets, or "troubadours," sing to the glory of these brave men. Richard built his adult life around these early loves of his childhood—fighting and poetry. Even in the harsh war camps of his Crusader campaign, Richard wrote poetry and kept troubadours in his retinue.

His father could never decide how to divide his vast properties among his sons. Eleanor gave Aquitaine to her beloved Richard, but her sons fought each other — and their father — over land and titles. Even John, his favorite son, turned against Henry, and the old king died alone, cursing his children. Richard, his oldest living son, inherited Henry's realms.

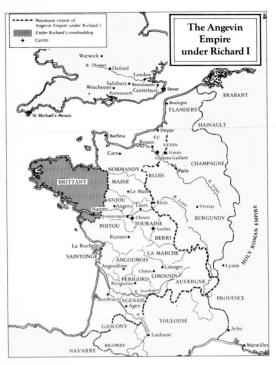

The Angevin
Empire
under Richard I

- - - Maximum extent of Angevin Empire under Richard I
▨ Under Richard's overlordship
♦ Castles

ANGEVIN EMPIRE
(left) The heart of the Angevin Empire inherited by Richard I was Anjou in France, where Richard's family came from.

RICHARD'S CORONATION
in London (right) was a magnificent affair.

CYPRUS (below) *became a Crusader stronghold when Richard conquered the island in 1191.*

The Fotomas Index

an afterlife in hell.

As soon as he raised the money, King Richard I of England gave his brother John authority to rule in his absence, and then he persuaded Philip II of France to join him in the war against the Muslims. Richard left Dover to meet up with Philip in France, and the two Kings swore in the great cathedral of Vezelay to support each other on crusade. Together, with their bands of knights, wagons, and horses, they started the long journey to Jerusalem.

The Lionheart loved war and he was in battle long before he reached the Holy Land. He fought King Tancred in Messina, Sicily, and conquered the King of Cyprus, the Greek Byzantine Isaac Comnenus. An honorable, stern man, Richard controlled his troops through harsh rules and was merciless to prisoners-of-war. Then he would

Sonia Halliday

RELIGIOUS FERVOR drove many to go on the Crusades. They hoped to avoid hell (below left) by fighting for Christ.

He went to Westminster to be crowned King of England, but used the occasion to raise money to go on a Crusade, a holy war, to save Jerusalem from the Muslims. He said he would sell London if it helped pay for the Crusade. Richard, a religious man like many kings before him, believed that every Crusader would be blessed by God and given a place in heaven when they died. He wanted to be the greatest Crusader King, and he did not dare to risk

Giraudon

A King for Ransom

In December, 1192, Richard the Lionheart was captured and imprisoned while traveling through the lands of Leopold, Duke of Austria. Leopold was seeking revenge because Richard had humiliated him by having his banner cast down off the walls of the city of Acre after its capture. Richard did this because Leopold—a mere Duke—had placed his banner beside those of the Kings of England and France.

Richard hoped to avoid capture by being disguised as a poor Knight Templar. But one night in a tavern, someone spotted the large ruby ring he wore. It was not the type of jewelry to be worn by a humble Knight Templar; Richard was taken prisoner.

After capturing his prize, Leopold kept Richard in various castles before sending him to the castle of Dürnstein on the Danube. Legend records how a wandering minstrel called Blondel searched for his King by traveling from castle to castle playing a song that only he and Richard knew. Eventually, he came to the walls of Dürnstein Castle. He sang the song; Richard heard him and sang it back from inside the castle. Thus, Blondel discovered the King's exact location. The story is highly improbable, but a song actually written by Richard when in prison does still exist. It's called "Ja Nus On Pris" and it describes his feelings at being neglected.

Leopold demanded a huge ransom of 100,000 marks—worth more than $6 million today. Richard's mother Eleanor and his loyal English subjects worked hard to raise the money and finally managed it, despite constant interference from John, Richard's younger brother, who wanted desperately to become king.

repent of his cruelty, and in Sicily, he sought guidance from the holy Hermit Joachim. Richard made the priests whip him for his sins as he crawled through Messina.

His adoring mother joined him in Cyprus and brought him a bride, Berengaria of Navarre, whose brother had agreed to protect Aquitaine during the Crusade. The girl went to Jerusalem with Richard, but he neglected her for the pleasure of war and fighting.

Richard the Lionheart was a curious mixture of cruelty and high idealism. Despite his brutality, his soldiers loved him for his bravery and fairness. Even Saladin, the great Muslim warrior, admired the Lionheart and said he was glad that the noble Richard, and no other Christian, had defeated him in battle.

However, Philip and other Crusade leaders learned to hate Richard, and the Crusade was not entirely successful. The English King was often ill, and there were times when Christian soldiers had to eat grass, so badly did they suffer from starvation. And Richard never entered Jerusalem. Exhausted by battle, and having made a treaty with Saladin, he knew he could not fight any more. So he refused to look upon the Holy City.

His journey home was difficult. Leopold of Austria, angered by Richard's scorn in Acre, hunted him down

The Mansell Collection

RICHARD'S DEATH
Richard was killed by a bolt from a crossbow. As he lay dying, he asked to see the crossbowman and forgave him, ordering his release. But, after Richard's death, the man was hanged.

RESTING PLACE
(left) Richard's tomb lies in the Abbey of Fontevrault, Anjou.

NATIONAL HERO
(right) Richard's statue is outside the Houses of Parliament in London.

and imprisoned him. But the English adored their warrior king and paid a huge ransom for his safe travel through Europe. Besides, they hated his weak, greedy brother, John. Richard landed at Sandwich, and the people welcomed him in London. He went through a grand ceremony in Winchester, where, surrounded by his nobles and followed by his subjects, he led a holy procession to the cathedral.

But his real love was for the Plantagenet domains of Anjou and Aquitaine, and he was soon back in France. Home at last, Richard relaxed and indulged his taste for music and art. This unusual soldier took great pleasure in decorating and furnishing his princely homes. His great skill as an architect was expressed in the severe beauty of his fortress and castle, Chateau Gaillard. He found time during the design and construction of his new property to conduct the music and the choir singing in the local church.

However, not all France was glad to see the Plantagenet lord back in his domains. His old crusading comrade, Philip, was now his sworn enemy.

Soon, Richard was skirmishing with his local lords and the King of France, enjoying

his favorite pastime—war.

Part of Richard's luck and skill as a medieval knight was due to the unusual length of his arms. He had an advantage in the close, quick flurry of sword battles when he could swiftly thrust his weapon into an enemy before he himself was in danger. But against a distant bowman, Richard had no resources. During a minor skirmish in Chalus, a crossbow bolt struck him, and the wound became infected.

Yet, even on his death bed, Richard proved himself "the most noble knight" and forgave the man who killed him. It was this fierce creed of honor and courage that earned him the title of Richard the Lionheart and a heroic place in history.

THE DEFEAT OF SALADIN

A brilliant commander, Richard showed at the battle of Arsuf that the mighty Saladin could be beaten.

The night of June 8, 1191, saw an amazing sight near the port of Acre, on the coast of the Holy Land. The red glare of bonfires and torches showed Crusader soldiers singing and dancing, with the sound of trumpets, horns, flutes, and bells traveling far in the warm, sweet-scented air.

From a distance, grimly silent, the men of the Muslim leader Saladin watched the proceedings. They knew that they had a fight on their hands. For nearly two years, they had been besieging the Christian encampment outside Acre, who in turn were besieging the Muslim garrison in the port. Neither side could completely prevent supplies from getting through to the other, and the situation had reached stalemate.

Only a day or so earlier, a great ship laden with supplies for the Muslim garrison had

The Hutchinson Library

THE HEAT OF THE DESERT made fighting difficult for the European Crusaders.

been sunk. It was said that also on board had been 200 venomous snakes, which would have been released in the Christian camp to create havoc. Now, the man whose massive fleet had sunk that vessel was joining forces and celebrating with the be-

Ronald Sheridan

RICHARD I

SALADIN (above), leader of the Muslim forces, proved his power by capturing Jerusalem. It was to free the Holy Land from the Muslims that Christians embarked on Crusades (left).

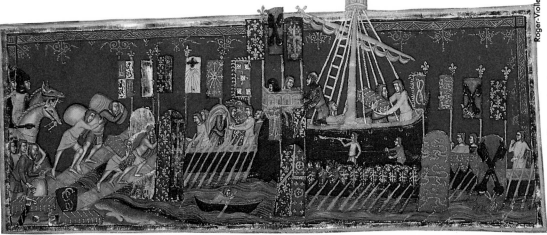

Sonia Halliday

Roger-Viollet

33

leaguered Christian forces. Richard the Lionheart had arrived.

Richard's arrival made all the difference to the Christian forces. They were the remnant of the army of Guy, the King of Jerusalem, whom Saladin had defeated at the Battle of Hattin three years before. The brave monk-knights in the orders of the Templars and Hospitallers, whose lives were pledged to defend Jerusalem, had all been slain. Guy had been captured then, but

eventually was released by Saladin after swearing that he would no longer fight. Guy swiftly broke his promise and, in a last bid to hold onto territory, had besieged Acre. The Christian army there had been swelling ever since, as Crusaders arrived from all over Europe.

Things moved quickly once Richard arrived. He took control and used his fleet to blockade the port of Acre so no fresh supplies could get into the beleaguered city. After more than two years, the defenders were ex-

hausted, and seeing their supply lines cut by Richard's fleet and the new energy he brought to the fight, they surrendered on July 12, 1191, little more than a month after Richard arrived on the scene.

After the fall of Acre, Philip—King of France—went home. This left Richard as commander of the whole Crusader army. His aim now was to liberate Jerusalem. But first, he had to march south to Jaffa. Taking Jaffa would give him a secure base, with access to the sea,

from which he could plan his campaign and conduct his attack against Jerusalem itself. The march to Jaffa would be dangerous, and Richard knew that the Crusaders would be harried and attacked all the way by Saladin's forces.

To get around the problem, Richard marched the Crusader army out of Acre in tight formation. He ordered his forces to march close to the seashore so the right flank was protected by the sea, and Richard's ships

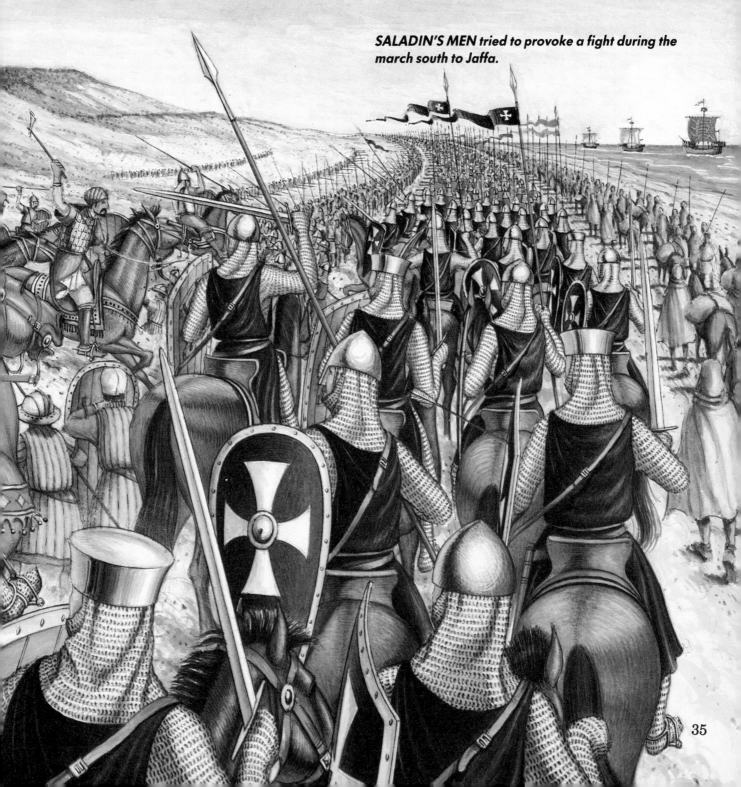

SALADIN'S MEN *tried to provoke a fight during the march south to Jaffa.*

35

FORTIFIED CASTLES were built by Crusaders to defend their territory in the Holy Land.

could constantly re-supply the army.

Saladin's forces started their attacks almost as soon as the Crusaders started their march. Hordes of light cavalry and archers made swooping attacks on the left flank, and the Hospitallers in the rear were mercilessly harried. To the Muslims, high on the ridge, the army looked like a giant, lumbering caterpillar. Day after day, Saladin ordered his forces into the attack, while the Crusader knights rode in full armor. Richard himself was wounded in the leg by an arrow, but ignored it. Saladin realized that his only chance was to force a pitched battle. He chose as his battleground the plain north of Arsuf.

The real action began in mid-morning of September 7, 1191, with an all-out attack by the Muslims on the rear guard of Hospitallers. The Turks—almost 10,000 strong—hurled themselves at the knights, throwing javelins and shooting arrows. Other sections of Saladin's forces, including Saracens and Bedouins, came forward, and the clashing of cymbals and Turkish drums was dreadful. The rain of arrows was so thick that some said it blotted out the sunlight.

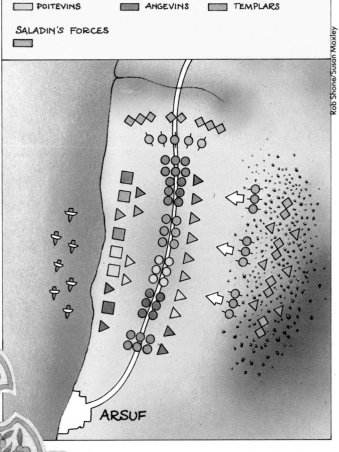

BATTLE OF ARSUF

● CAVALRY   ◉ MOUNTED TURKISH ARCHERS   ⚓ RICHARD'S FLEET

◆ HEAVY CAVALRY   ▲ INFANTRY   ■ BAGGAGE

RICHARD'S FORCES
- HOSPITALLERS
- POITEVINS
- FRENCH
- ANGEVINS
- ANGLO-NORMANS
- TEMPLARS

SALADIN'S FORCES

ARSUF

***THE BATTLE OF ARSUF (left)** The Crusader army kept close to the sea for protection. Provoked by Saladin's forces, the knights charged and swept Saladin back.*

THE SOLDIERS
Normally on horseback, this Seljuk Turk (left) is firing an arrow. His chest armor is made of metal plates. A Knight Templar (right) carries the banner of his order. Next to him (center right) is a Knight Hospitaller in his somber garb and great helmet. Far right is a knight in the battle-dress of the Third Crusade.

The Grand Master of the Hospitallers twice asked for permission to charge, and Richard refused. But the Hospitallers' patience was worn out. An English Hospitaller—Baldwin Carew—spurred his horse forward in a singlehanded attack. His brother knights immediately followed him, with their Grand Master at their head. The Hospitallers charged moments before Richard ordered a general attack. Days of pent-up frustration and anger were unleashed as the knights lowered their lances, turned towards their enemies, and spurred their horses forward. The charge of the combined Crusader divisions was so fierce that the Muslim forces were swept back. Muslim counterattacks on the English guarding Richard's standard were brushed aside. Saladin's demoralized forces turned about and retreated to the protection of the wooded areas around Arsuf. The Crusaders resumed their march in high spirits.

As a battle, the outcome was inconclusive, but to the Crusaders, it was a great victory. Several thousand Muslims were slain, including 32 Emirs. Richard's losses were less than 700, including only one nobleman. The mighty Saladin was not invincible.

Richard, despite further success, never realized his ultimate dream—he failed to recapture Jerusalem. He had neither the manpower nor resources. But, before his departure, he signed a treaty that secured the survival of the Christian Kingdom for another 100 years.

THE THIRD CRUSADE
1189 *Richard I of England, Philip of France, and Frederick Barbarossa, Holy Roman Emperor, raise armies to rescue Jerusalem.*
1190 *Richard and Philip set sail from Marseilles. Barbarossa is drowned, and the German army destroyed in Cilicia.*
1191 *Richard and Philip arrive at Acre and recapture the city. Philip leaves the Holy Land. Battle of Arsuf.*
1192 *Battle of Jaffa. Richard fails to recapture Jerusalem. Treaty between Richard and Saladin gives security to the Kingdom of Jerusalem and safe passage to pilgrims. Richard leaves the Holy Land.*
1193 *Saladin dies.*

Michael Holford

A CRUSADER TOMB often had an effigy of a knight with legs crossed and about to draw his sword.

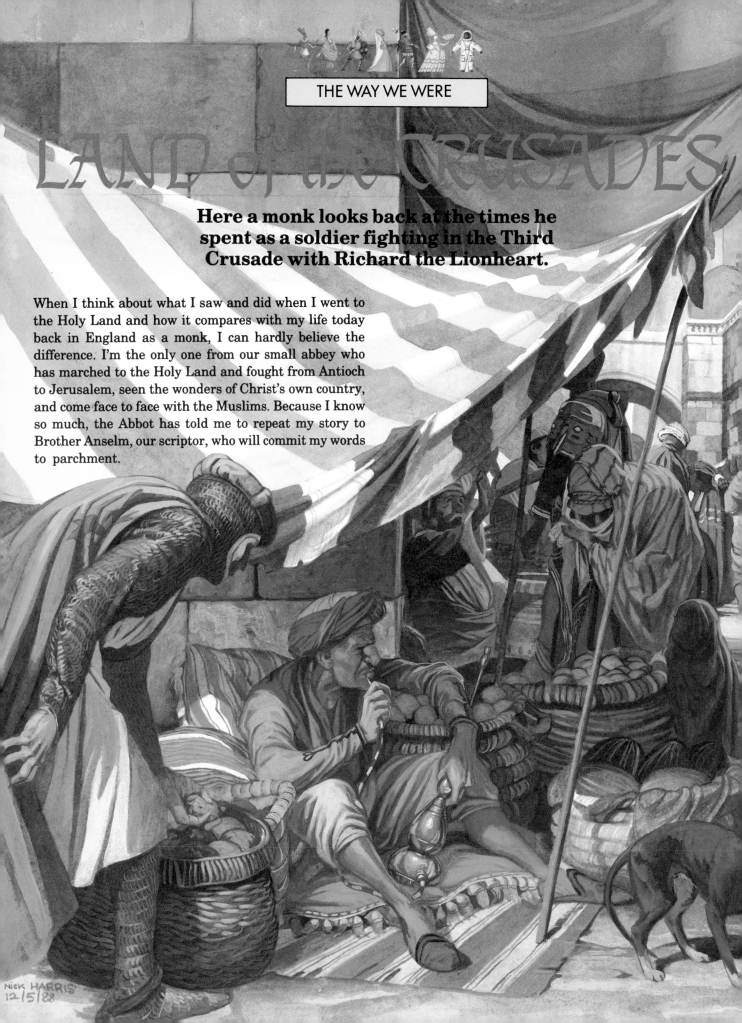

LAND of the CRUSADES

Here a monk looks back at the times he spent as a soldier fighting in the Third Crusade with Richard the Lionheart.

When I think about what I saw and did when I went to the Holy Land and how it compares with my life today back in England as a monk, I can hardly believe the difference. I'm the only one from our small abbey who has marched to the Holy Land and fought from Antioch to Jerusalem, seen the wonders of Christ's own country, and come face to face with the Muslims. Because I know so much, the Abbot has told me to repeat my story to Brother Anselm, our scriptor, who will commit my words to parchment.

But I'm rushing ahead a bit in my story. I'd better say how the whole situation came about. Men have been "Taking the Cross" — swearing an oath to go on a crusade — for the last hundred years or so. To begin with, it was to rescue Jerusalem from the Muslim Turks. That was way back in my great-grandfather's time — less than 30 years after the Battle of Hastings. People used to go on pilgrimages to Jerusalem, but the Muslims put a stop to all that. So, the pope at that time, Urban, made a famous plea that Jerusalem should be in Christian hands.

All over Europe, people responded. The great princes and dukes led their armies overland to Constantinople, then to Antioch, and finally recaptured Jerusalem itself. After this success, they set up the Christian Kingdom of Jerusalem with Frankish rulers from northern Europe.

Nick Harris

Unfortunately, things have not gone well recently. The ruler of the Kingdom of Jerusalem, that worthless King Guy, has let things go from bad to worse. First, he lost Jerusalem to Saladin, the Muslim leader, and then he allowed his whole Christian army to be overrun. After this, new appeals went out through the West for the great leaders once more to rescue the Holy Land. I myself heard the Archbishop of Canterbury when he toured Wales and the border country to raise men to accompany King Richard on his great crusade. I was fired with a desire and a will to wield my sword in the name of Christ. One reason was that all who go on a crusade receive everlasting absolution. This means that

EXOTIC LIFE

Burrell Collection

CRAFT SKILLS
One of the things that Crusaders saw were the beautiful colored tiles (left) commonly used to decorate walls inside and outside Arab buildings.

Courtesy of Sotheby's

PLANTS AND FRUITS
There were many new tastes for Christians on Crusades. These included pepper, poppy seed, and garlic (left). They also could try many exotic dried fruits.

RUGS AND CARPETS
Europeans were used to rush flooring, so Oriental carpets seemed luxurious (below).

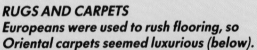

I'll go straight to heaven when I die, and all my sins are automatically forgiven.

The story of my journey overland to the Holy Land, with two companions, would need a book to itself. The only thing that kept us going, as we traveled eastward through the Holy Roman Empire that covers half of Europe, was the knowledge that countless others from many other lands were doing the same thing. We met up with the armies of the English and French kings at Acre. Our travels had taken us two full years.

I fought by the King's side at the siege of Acre, then on the march south through Arsuf, and at Jaffa. I made new friends over the months, but many of them died,

ARAB SCRIBE
Crusaders were amazed at the standard of learning of their Moslem foes. They not only had a different alphabet, but also a better way of counting. The numbers they used were eventually adopted in the West.

either from battle wounds or from disease.

The weather was so different, and our rough clothes gave us little comfort from the dry heat of the day and bitter cold of the night. When I first saw our enemy, I was amazed at the way they dressed — long flowing robes of bright silk with high wound turbans. But I soon learned that the garments and dress of our enemies were perfect for the climate; as they were light and airy, the layers protected them from the sun's heat and kept them warm through the long cold nights. As soon as I could, I started wearing Muslim clothes and felt much better after that.

In fact, I learned a lot about the Muslims and got to

HOLY BOOK
The Koran is the sacred book of the Muslim faith (left). The pages are often decorated.

MELON SELLER
Melons are grown in the Holy Land. The woman selling them (right) is dressed according to the customs of the Muslim religion.

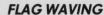

ARAB ASTRONOMERS
The Arabs studied the heavens and built observatories (below) to measure the stars.

NAVIGATION AID
The Arabs used astrolabes (above) to find out their exact location by the position of objects in the sky.

FLAG WAVING
This group of horsemen (above) are the standard bearers of the Caliph of Baghdad. They carry flags and pennants, and are playing trumpets and drums which, in battle, produce noise to terrify their enemies. Caliphs are said to be descendants of Mohammed.

understand their ways. Like us, they were on a religious quest of their own, to spread the word of Mohammed the Prophet. Muslims believe in one God as we do, one they call Allah, and in many ways, they are not unlike us in their religious zeal.

I had heard tales that they were barbaric and cruel and tortured their enemies. On the field of battle, they were indeed brave and ferocious. But in times of peace, they were ever courteous and once they gave their word, I never knew them to break it. To our shame, they treated their captives with far more consideration than we ever did. In truth, there was much that we from the Christian world could learn from them.

There were long periods between battles when Richard was negotiating for a firm and lasting peace with Saladin, and I spent the time learning much about what I saw around me. I was impressed. For instance, the Muslims were skilled in arithmetic and writing — they used an alphabet totally unlike ours. Also, they built fine houses that were airy, with marble mosaic floors. They were very skilled in the arts of healing — one of my interests — and I returned home with many new plants and skills in medicine. Because of this, I am now considered something of an apothecary.

I tasted all kinds of new foods and spices and, like many knights, returned home to the West carrying fine silks, spices, delicate soft woods, and many herbs.

Our King never managed to free Jerusalem, and he wept at his failure. But he did come to an agreement with Saladin that the Holy City was once again to be opened to Christian pilgrims. The King himself refused to enter the city and averted his eyes when near it, vowing that if he could not free the city from the Muslim yoke, then he would never look upon the City of Christ.

I never saw our King after he departed, as I stayed another three years before coming home. The fighting, heat, and fevers I experienced in the Holy Land have left me weakened, but the wonders of the East will forever remain strong in my memory.

HOLY PLACES OF JERUSALEM

DOME OF THE ROCK
Legend has it that the cupola (below), now of aluminum, was once covered in pure gold.

Sonia Halliday

Courtesy of Sotheby's

JERUSALEM is holy to people of all faiths. Below, a muezzin calls Muslims to prayer at the mosque.

MOUNT OF OLIVES This Crusader chapel marks where Christ is believed to have ascended to heaven.

Michael Holford

THE WAILING WALL (above) is a reminder to the Jews of the destruction of their Second Temple in A.D. 70. It is part of the wall which surrounded the Temple complex, and is still a major Jewish holy place.

The Hutchinson Library

Sonia Halliday

THE CHURCH OF THE HOLY SEPULCHER (top) was built by the Crusaders in 1149. Its dome is a landmark of Jerusalem. Inside, (bottom), lies the tomb where Christ is supposed to have been buried.

42

King John

When Richard I died, he was succeeded by his younger brother, John, who could not have been a more different man. Richard had been a chivalrous soldier whose ease of manner had made him a popular king. John easily offended his powerful barons, who remembered his failures in Ireland and his disloyalty to Richard. John was certainly treacherous, untrustworthy, and weak, but he was also a cultured man and an effective administrator. "Bad King John" was not uniquely evil, and there were to be other rulers who could, with better qualifications, compete for the title of worst king in English history.

King John

The "worst king in English history" or a misunderstood monarch? Judge for yourself!

Peter Roberts

King John has gone into the history books as a terrible tyrant and one of the most evil kings in the history of England. But was he really as bad as he has been painted? Many records dated from John's reign still exist, and they give an insight into his true character. Some are accurate and reliable, but others, such as the chronicles of Matthew Paris and Roger of Wendover, were embroidered for the sake of a good story.

Born in Oxford on Christmas Eve, 1167, John was the eighth and youngest child of

the infamous "Devil's Brood" of Henry II and Eleanor of Aquitaine. Like his brother, the great warrior Richard the Lionheart, he was wild and undisciplined as a child. Both his Plantagenet parents were strong-willed, energetic people with fiery tempers. They were constantly fighting with each other and with the rest of their family. Legend had it that the Plantagenets were descended from the daughter of Satan, which gave rise to the "Devil's Brood" nickname.

John grew up a feckless, irresponsible youth, always in the shadow of his father Henry and his brother Richard I. He inher-

Personal Profile

KING JOHN
Born *December 24, 1167.*
Died *October 18, 1216.*
Reign *1199-1216.*
Parents *Henry II and Eleanor of Aquitaine.*
Personal appearance *About 5'5" tall, well-built, and said to be dark-skinned and ugly. Careful about his appearance; liked jewelry.*
General *A passionate hunter and fond of luxurious living; said to enjoy sleeping late. He could be suspicious, bad-tempered, and cruel to barons who might stand in his way, but could be generous to those who served him well.*

Edimedia

ELEANOR of Aquitaine (left) was the remarkable mother of Richard the Lionheart and of King John. She exerted a strong influence on both her royal sons.

ANGERS (right), in the English domain of Anjou, was an important fortress which John defended successfully against an attack by King Philip II of France, only to lose it in 1214 to Prince Louis of France.

Burgerbibliothek, Bern

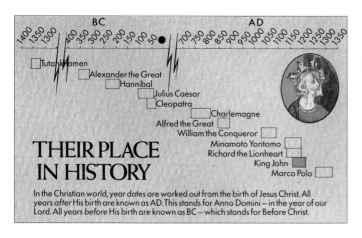

THEIR PLACE IN HISTORY

BC — AD

1400 1350 1300 · 400 350 250 200 150 100 50 · 700 750 800 850 900 950 1000 1050 1100 1150 1200 1250 1300 1350

Tutankhamen

Alexander the Great
Hannibal
Julius Caesar
Cleopatra
Charlemagne
Alfred the Great
William the Conqueror
Minamoto Yoritomo
Richard the Lionheart
King John
Marco Polo

In the Christian world, year dates are worked out from the birth of Jesus Christ. All years after His birth are known as AD. This stands for Anno Domini — in the year of our Lord. All years before His birth are known as BC — which stands for Before Christ.

ited all the energy and unpleasantness of the Plantagenets, but sadly, he had none of the charm so characteristic of his father and brother.

Several events marred the young prince's life. He had always been something of a problem for his father, who had four healthy sons and knew that only one could inherit the crown. As a solution, Henry planned to divide up his lands so each of his sons could rule a portion. John, who was the youngest, was made Lord of Ireland, and in 1185 Henry sent him to crush a rebellion. The 19-year-old John failed miserably in his attempt and returned to England to face disgrace and ridicule.

Just a few years after this disaster, John's father and his two eldest brothers were dead, and Richard was crowned king. Richard spent much of his reign fighting the Crusades, and in his absence, John tried to usurp his position and assume the role of king. When Richard returned from the Holy Wars, he found John hiding in France and forgave him, making John, who was then 27 years old, look cowardly and foolish.

Richard died in battle in 1199, and when John came to

Ronald Sheridan

Sonia Halliday

CONSTANT WAR
During John's reign, England fought war after war, and the cost in money—and lives—was high.

HENRY II (left) *father of John mourns at the tomb of St. Thomas à Becket following his murder.*

the throne, his unfortunate reputation came with him. The first years of his reign were shadowed with the suspicion that he had murdered his young nephew, Arthur, who was his dead brother Geoffrey's son and his closest rival to the throne. No proof has ever come to light, but it is certain that Arthur disappeared under mysterious circumstances while in John's care.

War between England and Philip of France raged almost constantly throughout John's reign. But, unlike Richard the Lionheart, who hardly ever visited England during his reign and regarded the country as merely a means of paying for his wars, John was a hardworking and energetic ruler when he was not on a campaign. He traveled the length and breadth of England and

HUNTING with dogs (above) was one of John's great pastimes.

GAILLARD Castle (left) fell to a French attack—a blow to John's prestige.

made sure that records were kept about the nation's finances, taxes, and custom duties. He tried to make the officials who collected this money and who presided over the courts honest and efficient, but little of this good work is recorded in the chronicles written after John's death. In fact, much of John's bad reputation stems from the fact that he was not as glamorous and romantic a figure as Richard. Instead, he was ill at ease and awkward in company, and he probably upset many of the nobles who had already lost much of their money during the reigns of Henry and Richard.

John married twice. His first wife was his second cousin, Isabella, to whom he was

betrothed at the age of nine. Theirs was a political marriage, and there was little fondness between them. When she produced no heirs, John divorced her, and in 1200, he married a young French princess called Isabelle. All accounts agree that he was madly in love with his bride.

John had always been a vain young man, and as king, he was able to indulge all of his passions. He was particular about personal cleanliness and took baths more often than most people in those days. But fine clothes and jewelry interested him most of all, and he owned vast quantities of both. He was cultivated in his tastes and fond of books— he always carried a small traveling library with him as he journeyed.

Perhaps the most curious aspect of his

King John's Fleet

When King John lost his lands in the north of France, he realized that England's first line of defense was the sea. Although he had a fleet of ships at his disposal on the south coast, they were only obliged to do 15 days service a year. So, with characteristic efficiency, John set to work constructing an artificial harbor at the tiny port of Portsmouth and building a fleet of fighting ships which would always be at his disposal. This fleet was added to and improved by later monarchs until it grew into the Royal Navy.

ISABELLE of Angoulême (left) was John's second wife. He married her to strengthen his position in France but it was also—unusually for the time—a genuine love match.

Mary Evans

character was his inconsistency. The nobles and clergy found him thoroughly disagreeable, greedy, and uncooperative, yet he was good to his household, whom he liked to see happy and well-fed. He found it impossible to get along with the barons and nobles whose support was necessary in order to run the country. Instead, he chose his friends and advisors from the lower ranks, with whom he felt more comfortable. He had a few loyal supporters among the nobility, notably William Marshal, Earl of Pembroke, who had been a great friend of John's father, Henry. Marshal proved to be equally loyal to

POPE INNOCENT III ordered John to return Church property and threatened to depose him. The French offered to help the Pope, but before they could invade England, John agreed to pay an annual fee to the Church in Rome.

John and supported him throughout his bitter wars and struggles.

Unlike his father and brother, John was unlucky in war. He lost Normandy to the French and had difficulty controlling the other areas of France over which he was lord. At home in England, he made the grave mistake of disagreeing with Pope Innocent III about the choice of Archbishop of Canterbury, and this, coupled with John's acquisi-

Bodleian Library

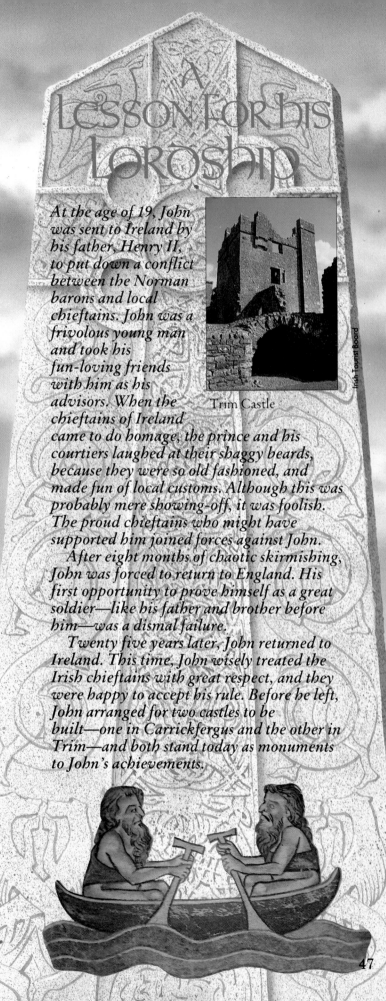

A LESSON FOR HIS LORDSHIP

At the age of 19, John was sent to Ireland by his father, Henry II, to put down a conflict between the Norman barons and local chieftains. John was a frivolous young man and took his fun-loving friends with him as his advisors. When the chieftains of Ireland Trim Castle

Irish Tourist Board

came to do homage, the prince and his courtiers laughed at their shaggy beards, because they were so old fashioned, and made fun of local customs. Although this was probably mere showing-off, it was foolish. The proud chieftains who might have supported him joined forces against John.

After eight months of chaotic skirmishing, John was forced to return to England. His first opportunity to prove himself as a great soldier—like his father and brother before him—was a dismal failure.

Twenty five years later, John returned to Ireland. This time, John wisely treated the Irish chieftains with great respect, and they were happy to accept his rule. Before he left, John arranged for two castles to be built—one in Carrickfergus and the other in Trim—and both stand today as monuments to John's achievements.

British Museum

KING JOHN *often traveled around England to ensure law and order in his realm.*

tion of church lands for personal gain, eventually led to a bitter feud with the clergy and John's excommunication. John had little interest in religion (although he did follow religious convention), but this situation posed a serious problem for the king.

Meanwhile, his demand for money to finance the wars in France made people increasingly angry, and the unrest eventually led to the signing of the Magna Carta—not only a momentous event in John's time, but one which had far-reaching consequences that still affect people in Britain today.

Unfortunately, the Magna Carta did not put an end to John's problems. Troubles with the English barons continued, and there were always new difficulties to confront. In September, 1216, John was forced to drive back the Scottish king, who had

Mansell

MARBLE EFFIGY *of King John covers the tomb in Worcester Cathedral where he was buried according to his wishes.*

WILLIAM MARSHAL *(above), a trusted friend.*

Ronald Sheridan

Giraudon

PHILIP of France.

John's Jewels

The famous medieval chronicler, Matthew Paris, told the tale of how disaster struck John and his household in October, 1216. Traveling in mist, the party fell into the quicksands of the Wash in East Anglia. Within minutes, the King's jewelry was lost forever.

Ronald Sheridan   Michael Holford

CASKET AND RING *from medieval times.*

marched with his army as far as Cambridge. Following this, the royal party took a short cut across the treacherous sands of the Wash, which proved to be a foolish mistake, as some of his baggage and servants were lost, swept away by the incoming tide. Writing long after the event, Matthew Paris exaggerated the story, claiming that John lost all his famous jewels (which he usually did carry with him). Few of the jewels John was known to possess were ever found—so there may be some truth in the story.

Following the loss, the depleted party pressed on to Newark in Nottinghamshire, and John, who had not been well for some time, became seriously ill. On October 18, he died, probably of dysentery. So ended the turbulent reign of the man whom some have called "the worst king in English history."

MAGNA CARTA

Out of the strife and turbulence of King John's reign came Magna Carta—the charter of liberties upon which English laws are based.

The beautiful June morning did nothing to improve King John's mood. He had waked up in Windsor that day in an extremely bad mood, and his unfortunate servants had borne the brunt of his discontent. Months of trying to suppress a handful of rebel barons had finally failed, so in order to keep hold of his crown—and possibly his life—he had been strongly advised by his friends and counsellors to put his royal seal upon a document which had been prepared by the discontented nobles.

John deeply resented the rebellion, for was he not king and ruler of all England? And why should the king be dictated to by such upstarts! As he mounted his horse and headed toward the field at Runnymede, he vowed to break every promise he was about to make to the barons.

As John approached the field, he could see that the barons and their servants had already gathered. Without doubt, this was a miserable day for John, but it was too late to change his mind now. He would just have to agree to their terms!

The problems between King John and his

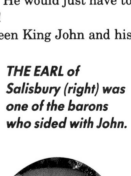

THE EARL of Salisbury (right) was one of the barons who sided with John.

Mary Evans

J Allan Cash

RUNNYMEDE, where John agreed to Magna Carta. A memorial marks the site. Carved on one pillar are words which sum up the significance of this great charter (inset).

J Allan Cash

barons began long before John came to the throne. At the very root of the trouble lay the feudal system, which had been introduced by William the Conqueror and was still in operation. The feudal system was based on the idea that every person in the land had a lord to whom he owed loyalty and certain services. At the top of this pyramid-like system was the king, and below him were the clergy and barons who owned a substantial amount of land. In return for this ownership, they became the king's "vassals" and swore obedience to the king. Known as tenants-in-chief, these men had the right to transfer land and other privileges to other tenants—usually knights—while, in return, the knights had to swear obedience and fight for their lords when necessary. Then came the "villeins," some of whom did duty in return for a small amount of land, while a very few of the lowliest serfs held no land but worked just for their food and shelter.

Although the king was overlord, he relied upon his powerful barons to provide men from their lands to fight in the royal army and help provide a steady income of money. This money was paid in the form of taxes to supplement the royal coffers—always emptied by expensive wars.

Nick Harris

For some years, the barons had been unhappy with the level of taxation. John's father, Henry II, had made great demands on the barons' resources in order to fund his European wars, and Richard I, his brother, asked for even more for his crusades. Although the barons were displeased with those claims, they remained loyal to the earlier kings because they won glorious battles and were seen to be strong and powerful rulers.

But, when John became king in 1199, things got worse. Many barons had reservations about the choice of John as ruler, as he had the reputation of being difficult and immature. As king, his inconsistent behavior toward his fellows did not improve.

Over the turbulent years of John's reign, he favored some barons by giving them land and pensions, while others got nothing at all. The northern barons particularly felt slighted by John's behavior. John also increased the amount of money and services that he demanded from his barons. Many landowners had to resort to borrowing cash at high rates of interest just to pay their dues for the king's wars. Naturally, their resentment increased when these wars were unsuccessful. On top of all this, John introduced new forms of taxation over and above the "scutage" (literally "shield money") that he could ask for in times of war. What finally sparked off the barons' revolt was John's demand for yet another increased rate of scutage in 1214. For the barons, this was the last straw!

Some 40 of the discontented nobles united and refused to submit any more to a king they considered disgraced and defeated in the wars with France. Encouraged by the Archbishop of Canterbury, Stephen Langton, they brought out a charter which had been drawn up many years ago and granted by King Henry I. It laid down rules concerning good government, and they wanted the king to confirm and abide by them in the future.

As opinion built up against the king, John tried to stall and pacify his opponents. But his angry barons were not to be appeased. John realized he would have to agree, even if only temporarily, to the barons' demands in order to hold onto his crown. Meetings were quickly arranged, and John agreed to see the barons on June 15, 1215, in a field on the banks of the River Thames near Windsor, where John was staying.

The event was not a joyous one for John and his supporters, but neither was it a victory for the barons,

IN FEUDAL SOCIETY, serfs form the basis, and above them are freemen and knights. The next layer includes lords and churchmen, with the king above everyone.

Rob Shone

The Burrell Collection

any way destroyed, nor will we proceed against or prosecute him except by the lawful judgment of his peers [equals] or by the law of the land." This clause was later interpreted as the right of every accused person in England to trial by a jury.

Today, Magna Carta is considered to be the foundation of English law. Many of the laws in use today are based on clauses that first appeared in Magna Carta, and generations of British children have learned a poem by Rudyard Kipling as a reminder that English liberty began at Runnymede:

Forget not after all these years
The charter signed at Runnymede
And still when Mob or Monarch lays
Too rude a hand on English ways
The whisper wakes, the shudder plays
Across the reeds at Runnymede.

as a lot of compromises had been made during the discussions. With great reluctance, John agreed to the terms, which restricted considerably his freedom of action as king. But the peace this brought was short-lived. Within months of the meeting at Runnymede, the king and his barons were squabbling again, and the barons continued their struggle to enforce the charter until the king's death in 1216.

The document came to be known as the Magna Carta, or "great charter," and it was re-issued on other occasions in history to restrict other kings. There were 63 clauses in all, which defined the rights of the people of England. One of its most famous clauses is the one that states: "No man shall be taken, imprisoned, outlawed, banished, or in

SERFS at work—even small children were involved.

COMMON LAW developed slowly in England. Magna Carta helped to define it.

Musee Municipal d'Avranche

Robin Hood

Robin Hood is one of England's most enduring legends, but the truth behind the myth has long been lost. Historians think that Robin Hood existed, but exactly who he was remains a mystery. Some say he was the aristocrat Robin of Locksley. Popular stories have Robin and his outlaws living in Sherwood forest, fighting for the people in the name of Richard the Lionheart against his evil brother, Prince John. He has always been portrayed as the hero who took from the rich to give to the poor.

Mander & Mitchenson

HIGH DAYS and HOLIDAYS

Festivals were the highlight of village life in medieval England, and one of the greatest was the harvest celebration. This is how it might have happened.

The sun is so hot today that if I could, I would run from the scorching fields down to the river and take a dip in the water to cool myself down. But tonight is the end of the harvest, and soon I must start work again to help cut the wheat in time for the celebrations. Everyone looks forward to harvest time in our village, even though we have been working from dawn well into the night under the harvest moon these last few weeks. The harvest celebrations give each family a chance to relax and enjoy themselves and forget all their cares and worries.

Life is not always easy for us farming folk. In our small village, there is often more work than we can cope with—sowing, reaping, cutting wood, and tending the cattle and sheep. But mostly we do all right. There is plenty of fresh air and usually enough food to go around.

Of course, our lives can't compare with those who live in the manor house. It has not long been built, and it is a fine, timber-framed house with a deep thatched roof and lots of space inside. They always have plenty to eat,

Graham Humphries

54

although in winter food is all salted and dried and not really much tastier than ours.

I can see the village from the hill where I am sitting, and I can see our house just on the edge. Our family is lucky enough to have a two-roomed house made from turf, with an outbuilding for the animals. Some families which are much larger than ours have to live in one room, and in winter they have all their animals in with them, which I wouldn't like at all. Now that I am 12, I get my own straw bed mat to sleep on, which is much better than sleeping with my small brother and sister!

This year, the harvest should be plentiful, which is a very good thing, as the last few years have not been very prosperous for our village. My father says that it is all because of King John, who is cruelly taxing the lord of our manor and forever making demands on him for fighting men, which seems unfair, as the king is really very rich and we have so little.

At least we still have some things to look forward to.

FLASH BACK

The Bridgeman Art Library

Birds and Beasts

FEUDALISM was built on rural life and agriculture and so animals played a vital role in medieval life. In a world without engines, cattle (below) were working beasts, pulling the plows for the serfs. Dogs were very important in the hunt (left). Artists were fascinated, and with great attention to detail and habitat, they depicted the wild creatures with loving care, as in the stained glass on the right.

British Library   Angelo Hornak

My little brother and sister were so excited about the harvest festival that they didn't sleep at all last night, but they don't realize how much planning the celebrations take. Ever since I can remember, Tom Tyler, the village steward, has taken care of most of the organization. Tom runs the manor for our lord, and although he works us hard, everyone considers him to be a good, kind, and fair man.

A few weeks ago, he gathered all the villagers together in order to plan the feast and choose the harvest queen. This year, my elder sister, who is just 13, was chosen; and ever since, she has been parading around with all the airs of the lady of the manor! I must admit we were all proud of her; to be chosen is a great honor. Tom's wife

has made her a new dress of white linen, which she is allowed to keep afterward. The dress is to be trimmed with lace (the very finest, my sister keeps saying) which Tom buys from a traveling merchant.

All the women are kept busy preparing special food, especially my mother, who makes the best gingerbread and seedcake in the village. All the food is carried to the manor barn where the feast is held, and already I can smell the delicious aroma of two oxen, which are being slowly roasted over a spit by the baker's wife.

Soon, we have to set to work on the last field, and once it is cut, the celebrations begin with the cutting of the "corn baby." The corn baby is really just the last sheaf of wheat in the field, which all the men cut together by

John Hilleleon/Roland Michaud

Ronald Sheridan

WOLVES, fierce and hungry, were feared throughout Europe, but in England they were almost extinct.

Aberdeen University Library

FALCONS trained to help people hunt their food would kill distant prey which was often collected by dogs. Crusaders brought back very fine Arab falcons (above). A page in a veterinary book on the care of ill dogs reveals how concerned medieval people were for the health of this animal, who was both friend and hunter. Paws and jaws caused a few problems, however (above right)!

ANIMALS were used for entertainment at fairs. Bear-baiting (below) was considered a very exciting pastime.

The Bridgeman Art Library

British Library

PORK was a staple food and was used in many ways—dried, salted, and cured.

throwing their sickles at it (it is considered bad luck for just one man to cut the corn baby). With a great cheer, the baby falls, and it is gathered up and presented to the harvest queen as her bouquet. Then, the harvest procession begins!

The harvest queen is hoisted up onto the haycart, which is drawn by a gentle chestnut horse whose mane is decorated with white ribbons. With garlands of fresh flowers in her hair, the queen holds the corn baby aloft so that everyone can see it. The corn baby is said to be the spirit of the harvest, and at the end of the celebrations, it must be placed into a special niche in the barn, where it rests until next year's harvest is brought in. All the villagers run beside the cart to reach the barn

in time for the "resting" ceremony, which is very important. When this year's corn baby is put in her place of honor, last year's baby is carried out and burned on a huge fire. Our parson says that this is just superstitious nonsense and a waste of time, but he grudgingly goes along with it, as one-tenth of the harvest always goes to the church (and he also likes a good feast like the rest of the villagers).

We are fortunate in our village to have a nearby spring, so we can drink fresh water as well as ale or cider. In many villages at this time of year, the wells and springs dry up and the little water they produce is unsafe to drink, so the villagers have no choice but to drink the local beer. Most of the adults in our village are

FLASH BACK

The Christian CALENDAR

Michael Holford

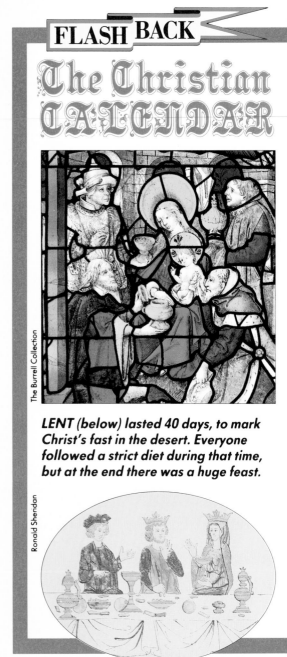

The Burrell Collection

Ronald Sheridan

CHRISTMAS (left) was a time for feasting and drinking, and the serfs were allowed a holiday.
EASTER (above) is a solemn time in church, and all the statues were draped with purple cloth.
MUSIC has always played an important part in church (right).

LENT (below) lasted 40 days, to mark Christ's fast in the desert. Everyone followed a strict diet during that time, but at the end there was a huge feast.

Ronald Sheridan

Edimedia

WEDDINGS were performed only in church (left), because the vows were made to God.

BAPTISM It was believed that to die unbaptized meant you would never go to heaven, so the ceremony was essential.

happy to drink ale all night long, although it makes them tipsy. Last year, I had to help pull old Matthew Marsh out of a ditch the morning after the harvest!

The feasting, drinking, and merrymaking goes on until dawn, and rightly so my father says, for in a few months, we shall have little to eat but dried and salted foods. Pease pudding and bacon are so boring! All the best food is saved for Christmas, when the celebrations and church-going go on for days.

Last year, my uncle was lucky enough to go to the Christmas banquet in the manor, and he said it was a very grand affair. Oxen, chickens, tiny larks, eggs, and

cakes flavored with strange spices brought all the way from the Holy Land were there to eat, as well as huge bowls laden with fruit and sweetmeats.

Our family loves Christmas, too, because after the fasting of Advent, it is wonderful to have special things to eat, such as a goose or capon and spicy mince pies, made from ground pork and herbs.

Once Christmas is over, it seems a long time until Easter, but there is sometimes a wedding or christening feast to cheer us through the long winter months.

Anyway, Tom Tyler is calling everyone to work, so I must go. I can't wait for the celebration to start!

GLOSSARY

Advent In the Christian Church calendar, the time period including the four Sundays before Christmas.

airs An affected manner; a show of pride.

Anglo-Saxon Of the Angle, Saxon or Jute peoples who ruled England before the Norman Conquest.

blockade To prevent passage to and from a place, using troops or ships as a barrier.

Breton A native of Brittany, in northern France.

capon A castrated and fattened chicken.

Cilica Ancient region in Asia Minor, now the south coast of Turkey.

coffers A treasury. Or, chests to hold money.

commissioner One given authority to do a task or execute business on behalf of an employer.

consecrate To make or declare sacred.

cultivated Refined; trained and developed.

Dark Ages Period in European history from the 5th to the 10th centuries, characterized by intellectual stagnation and widespread unrest.

devout Having or showing religious devotion.

dialect Local characteristics of speech.

domain The home or land one owns or rules.

dowry Property, money, or goods that a bride's family gives to her husband when she marries.

dynasty Rulers from the same family.

eisteddfod (Welsh) An assembly of bards and **minstrels**, where songs and poems are performed and exchanged.

Emir A Muslim military commander or ruler.

epic poem A long narrative poem about the deeds of a real or legendary hero.

epidemic A disease prevalent in a locality.

feudal system The economic, political and social organization of medieval Europe, in which land, worked by **serfs,** was held by **vassals** in exchange for services given to overlords.

Flanders Historical region of northern Belgium and bordering areas of France and the Netherlands.

fyrdsmen Members of the national Anglo-Saxon military force.

Sonia Halliday

gondola (Italian) A long, narrow canal boat.

habitat The natural home of a plant or animal.

Hospitallers A member of the monastic order, the Knights of St. John, founded in the 11th century to aid pilgrims in the Holy Land.

invest To install in office with ceremony.

legend A story handed down for generations, often believed to have a historical basis.

manor Land belonging to or under the authority of a lord, divided among peasants in return for rent or labor.

minstrel A traveling poet or singer.

miracle play A religious drama based on miracles performed by the saints.

mosaic Pictures or designs made by inlaying small bits of colored glass, stone, etc. into a surface.

mosque Islamic temple or place of worship.

Muslim A follower of Islam, the religion based on the teachings of the prophet Mohammed.

niche A recess or hollow in a wall.

Norsemen The ancient Scandinavian people.

pacify To calm; to make peace.

prefabricate To make or build in sections before assembly on a site.

press gang A group of men who round up other men and force them into military service.

prosperous Financially successful; thriving.

ransom The price paid or demanded for the release of a captive or of seized property.

rivet Nail or bolt for joining two pieces of metal.

schism A split or division in a group or society.

scribe A person who copied books by hand before printing was invented. In monasteries, scribes were called scriptors.

skirmish A short fight, between small groups of fighters, which is part of a bigger battle.

scutage Tax paid by a knight, often in lieu of military service.

serf In the **feudal system,** a person in servitude, bound to his master's land; a slave.

sickle A cutting tool with a short handle and a crescent-shaped blade, for cutting tall crops.

simony Buying or selling sacred relics.

sonnet A poem, usually of 14 lines in a fixed verse and rhyme scheme, expressing a single thought or idea.

tanner A person who tans animal hides into leather.

Templars A member of the monastic order, Knights Templar, founded in the 12th century to protect pilgrims on their way to and from the Holy Land.

thatch A roof covering of straw or rushes.

timber-framed Architecture style in which walls are built of wooden frames, filled with bricks or plaster.

tournament A series of jousting competitions in which mounted knights fought each other.

troubadour (French) A poet or poet-musician who wrote poems of love and chivalry.

turban A headdress consisting of a cap with a scarf wound around it.

turbulent Full of commotion or disturbance.

tyrant A cruel, oppressive leader.

usurp To take possession by force.

vassal In the **feudal system,** a tenant who performed a service for an overlord in return for land.

venemous Containing venom, a poisonous substance.

Viking One of the Scandinavian sea robbers and pirates of the 8th to 10th centuries.

villeins In the **feudal system,** a **serf** or peasant, entirely subject to a lord.

CHRONOLOGY

The Middle Ages 1050-1250

	POLITICS AND WAR	RELIGION AND PHILOSOPHY	
1050 to 1100	**1053** Norman knights conquer southern Italy. **1066** Edward the Confessor dies. Harold, Earl of Wessex, becomes King of England. Harold defeated by William of Normandy at the Battle of Hastings. William becomes William I of England. **1086** Domesday Book compiled. **1087** William I dies. His second son, William Rufus, becomes King of England. **1096** First Crusade begins to free the Holy Land from Muslim rule. **1099** Crusaders capture Jerusalem. Frankish states are founded in the Holy Land. **1100** William Rufus killed and is succeeded by his younger brother, Henry I.	**1052** Edward the Confessor begins building Westminster Abbey. **1054** Schism between Eastern and Western Catholic Churches becomes permanent. **1065** Westminster Abbey is consecrated. **1070** Order of St. John (the Hospitaller knights) founded in Jerusalem. **1075** Investiture Controversy begins between the Pope and Emperor over the right to invest bishops and abbots. **1080** Peter Abelard, theologian and philosopher, is born. **1095** Council of Clermont. Pope Urban II proclaims the First Crusade. **1098** First Cistercian monastery founded at Citeaux, France.	
1101 to 1150	**1120** *White Ship* disaster. Henry I's heir, William, is drowned. Matilda, Henry's other child, becomes heir. **1128** Matilda marries Geoffrey Plantagenet, Duke of Anjou. **1135** Henry I dies. His nephew, Stephen of Boulogne, seizes the throne. **1139-1148** Civil war in England between the supporters of Stephen and of Matilda. Matilda is defeated. **1144** The Turks retake the city of Edessa, captured by the first Crusaders. **1147-1149** Second Crusade fails to recapture Edessa.	**1115** Abbey of Clairvaux founded. St. Bernard is its first abbot. **1119-1120** Order of the Knights Templar founded in Jerusalem. **1122** Concordat of Worms ends the Investiture Controversy. **1123** First Lateran Council declares simony and the marriage of priests to be unlawful. **1137-1144** Abbot Suger builds the cathedral of St. Denis in Paris, the first great Gothic cathedral.	
1151 to 1200	**1152** Matilda's son, Henry, marries Eleanor of Aquitaine, former wife of the King of France. **1154** Henry succeeds Stephen as King Henry II of England and founds the Plantagenet dynasty. **1171** Saladin becomes Sultan of Egypt. **1172** Queen Eleanor rebels against Henry II. She is defeated and is imprisoned until 1185. **1187** Battle of Hattin. Saladin retakes Jerusalem. **1189** Henry II dies and is succeeded by his son, Richard I (the Lionheart). **1189-1193** Third Crusade fails to recapture Jerusalem, but a truce allows Christian pilgrims to enter the city. **1199** Richard I is killed in France. John, his younger brother, becomes King of England.	**1161** Edward the Confessor made a saint. **1162** Thomas à Becket, Henry II's Chancellor, is elected Archbishop of Canterbury. **1163-1235** Cathedral of Nôtre Dame is built in Paris. **1170** Thomas à Becket is murdered at Canterbury by four Norman knights. **1173** Thomas à Becket is made a saint. **1182** Francis of Assisi is born. **1190** Order of German Hospitallers founded. In 1198 it becomes the Teutonic Order.	
1201 to 1250	**1202-1204** Fourth Crusade. Western knights take Constantinople and found a Latin empire (1204-1261). **1204** England loses Normandy to France. **1212** Children's Crusade. Children from France and Germany set out to free Jerusalem. None reach the Holy Land. **1215** Magna Carta signed by King John. **1216** John dies. His son succeeds him as Henry III. **1217-1221** Fifth Crusade fails against Egypt. **1228-1229** Sixth Crusade. Emperor Frederick II negotiates a treaty by which Jerusalem is returned to Christian control. **1244** Muslims retake Jerusalem. **1248-1254** Seventh Crusade, led by St. Louis (Louis IX of France), fails against Egypt.	**1209-1229** Crusade against Albigensian heretics in southern France. **1210** Francis of Assisi issues the first rules of his new religious order, the Franciscans. **1212-1311** Reims Cathedral built in France. **1215** Dominican Friars founded by St. Dominic, a Spanish priest. **1225** Thomas Aquinas, theologian, philosopher and saint, is born. **1228** Francis of Assisi made a saint. **1231** Pope Gregory IX founds the Inquisition to discover and to try heretics.	

The Middle Ages were an era of bewildering contrast. While learning flourished in the new universities and peaceful saints like Francis of Assisi established their religious orders, knights from northern Europe fought fierce battles of conquest in southern Italy, in England and in the Holy Land.

ART AND LEARNING	SCIENCE AND SOCIETY	
1078 William I begins building the Tower of London. It is completed in c.1300. c.1088 Work begins on the Bayeux Tapestry. c.1100 In France, the dialect of the Ile-de-France (area north of Paris) becomes the dominant language. In England, Middle English takes over from Old English. c.1100 The *Chanson de Roland* (Song of Roland), French epic poem, is composed. c.1100 Polyphonic style develops in music.	c.1050 Astrolabes arrive in Europe from the East. 1066 A comet, later named Halley's Comet, is recorded. c.1070 Constantine the African brings Greco-Arab medicine to the attention of the West in his books. 1094 First record of the presence of gondolas in Venice, Italy. 1098 Nicholas Prevost writes *Antidotarium,* a collection of over 2,500 medical prescriptions.	1050 to 1100
1110 Earliest recorded miracle play performed in Dunstable, England. 1119 University founded at Bologna, Italy. c.1125 Beginning of troubadour music in France. 1136 Peter Abelard writes an account of his love affair with Heloise. 1144 French poet, Chrétien de Troyes, is born. 1147 Geoffrey of Monmouth writes his *History of the Kings of Britain.* 1150 Paris University founded.	1123 St. Bartholemew's Hospital is founded in London. 1133 St. Bartholemew's Fair is held in Smithfield, London, for the first time. (It is last held in 1855.) 1143 Benjamin of Tudela, a Spanish rabbi, travels to India and Egypt. 1150 A medical faculty is established at Bologna University. c.1150 Paper is manufactured by the Arabs of Spain.	1101 to 1150
1167 Oxford University founded in England. 1170 Chrétien de Troyes writes *Lancelot,* a romance of courtly love. 1174 The campanile (the "Leaning Tower") is built in Pisa, Italy. 1176 First eisteddfod held at Cardigan, Wales. 1176 The legends of King Arthur are arranged in their present form by Walter Map, an English poet. 1191 The *Nibelungenlied,* a German epic poem, is begun. 1197 Richard I of England builds Chateau Gaillard on the Seine River, France. 1200 Cambridge University founded in England. c.1200 Mississippi mound builders dominate North America. c.1200 Pueblo builders active in the American southwest.	c.1151 First recorded reference to insurance (against fire and plague in Iceland). 1151 The game of chess is first played in England. 1154 Mohammed al-Idrisi publishes his *Geography,* a collection of maps and geographical information. c.1170 First recorded epidemic of influenza in Europe. 1171 City of Belfast founded in Ireland. 1199 City of Liverpool founded in England.	1151 to 1200
1203 *Parzival* written by Wolfram von Eschenbach, German epic poet. 1210 Gottfield von Strassburg writes *Tristan und Isolde.* c.1220 Sonnet form develops in Italian poetry. 1240 Florentine painter Cimabue is born. 1248 Work begins on the Alhambra in Granada, Spain. c.1250 High Gothic period begins in German art.	1202 Leonardo Pisano Fibonacci introduces Arabic numbers to the West in his book *Liber abaci.* 1204 City of Amsterdam founded in Holland. 1214 Roger Bacon, great English scientist, is born. c.1225 Cotton cloth first manufactured (in Spain). 1230 City of Berlin founded in Germany. 1249 Roger Bacon describes the existence of explosives.	1201 to 1250

FURTHER READING

Ahsan, M.M., *Muslim Festivals*. Rourke Corp. (Vero Beach, 1987)

Atkinson, Ian, *The Viking Ships*. Lerner Publications (Minneapolis, 1980)

Barlow, Frank, *Thomas Becket*. University of California Press (Berkeley, 1986)

Baumgartner, Frederic J., *Henry II*. Duke University Press (Durham, 1988)

Brooks, Polly S., *Queen Eleanor: Independent Spirit of the Medieval World: a Biography of Eleanor of Aquitaine*. Harper & Row Junior Books (New York, 1983)

Davies, G.R., *Magna Carta*. Longwood Publishing Group (Wolfeboro, 1982)

Gee, Robin, ed., *Living in Castle Times*. EDC Publishing (Tulsa, 1982)

Gibb, Christopher, *Richard the Lionheart and the Crusades*. Watts, Franklin (New York, 1985)

Gillingham, John, *The Life and Times of Richard I*. Biblio Distribution Center (Totowa, 1973)

Jones, J.A., *King John and the Magna Carta*. Longman (White Plains, 1971)

Kaplan, Zoe, *Eleanor of Aquitaine*. Chelsea House (Edgemont, 1986)

Khattab, Huda, *(Muslim World*. Silver, Burdett & Ginn (Lexington, 1987)

Lane, Peter, *Norman England*. David & Charles (North Pomfret, 1980)

May, Robin, *William the Conqueror and the Normans*. Watts, Franklin (New York, 1985)

Miquel, Pierre, *Castles of the Middle Ages*. Silver, Burdett & Ginn (Lexington 1985)

Nichol, Jon, *King John*. Longman (White Plains, 1974)

Nichol Jon, *The First and Third Crusades*. Longman (White Plains, 1974)

Peach, L. Dugarde, *William the Conqueror*. Ladybird of Maine (Lewiston, 1956)

Scott, Walter, *Ivanhoe*. Silver Burdett & Ginn (Lexington, 1984)

Williams, Ann, *The Crusades*. Longman (White Plains, 1975)

Bridgeman

INDEX

Mary Evans